Ultimat
Comprehension Guide!

<u>Reading Comprehension</u>

Beginners Techniques For How To Improve Your Reading Comprehension, Reading Skills, And Speed Reading Fast!

Ryan Cooper

STOP!!! Before you read any further....Would you like to know the Success Secrets of how to make Passive Income Online?

If your answer is yes, then you are not alone. Thousands of people are looking for the secret to learning how to create their own online passive income style business.

If you have been searching for these answers without much luck, you are in the right place!

Because I want to make sure to give you as much value as possible for purchasing this book, right now for a limited time you can get 3 incredible bonuses for free.

At the end of this book I describe all 3 bonuses. You can access them at the end. But for those of you that want to grab your bonuses right now. See below.

Just Go Here For Free Instant Access:

www.OperationAwesomeLife.com/FreeBonuses

Legal Notice

Disclaimer Notice

Table Of Contents

Introduction

I want to thank you and congratulate you for purchasing the book, *"Reading Comprehension: Ultimate Reading Comprehension Guide! – Beginner's Techniques For How To Improve Your Reading Comprehension, Reading Skills, And Speed Reading Fast!"*

This "Reading Comprehension" book contains proven steps and strategies on how to improve your level of reading comprehension and master the skills that should go with it. You will be brushed up with the basics and as you go along with your reading, you will realize that things get a bit more complicated. Once you are ready, you can truly tackle items involving critical thinking.

Each of the chapters in this book gives sufficient explanation. Of course, you need to read in order to learn how to read, so it is essential to read this book from cover to cover. The skills presented in this compendium are actually very practical; therefore, you can readily apply them in any reading situation. There are very useful and very pragmatic suggestions. In the end, the goal here is to create an active reader in you.

Thanks again for purchasing this book, I hope you enjoy it!

Chapter 1–Understanding The Basics Of Reading

Reading is an important communication skill that each person – student, professional, and everything in between – should gain mastery of. It is said that reading is considered as the key that is meant to unlock the door of the world that is filled with mysteries, enjoyment, and enlightenment. For any content field, according to developmental reading researchers, reading is the most important tool in acquiring information. That information can then be processed so that it can become useful knowledge.

In our everyday life, eight out of the ten things that we involve ourselves in usually entail reading. From reading the signs that can be found on the street, down to the simple leisure surfing on the Internet, you need to read somehow. You also have to apply your reading skills when you are visiting any restaurant because you have to scan through their menu, and of course, if you wish to learn a new skill, you need to read your newly-purchased self-help eBook.

It is impossible for you to learn about the different famous and historical people, places you have never been to, and things that you have not seen yet, if you do not know how to read effectively. And yes, reading is also essential for having fun and getting involved in relaxation activities. After all, light reading, enjoying fiction, browsing through the comics, and engaging yourself in social media involve a great deal of reading.

In the past, reading was not seen as a major mode of acquiring knowledge. It was merely seen in the past decades as a leisure and recreational activity. But today, with the changes brought about by technology and with the rise of the World Wide Web and other digital technologies, there has been a renewed interest on knowledge. Every single day, new bits of information are readily available. If you will not read up, you will be left behind. With the explosion of available knowledge and the recent advancement in the field of technology and science, the skill of efficient reading has truly become a necessity.

In order to fully develop one's ability to read in the most efficient way possible, practice, as well as understanding, is needed. Adequate amount of practice will help you develop the needed skills in reading.

To get started, you need to learn and understand the basics of reading. There are three main techniques that may be used in reading, namely scanning, focused reading, and skimming. We will discuss each one by one.

Main Reading Technique #1: Scanning

Scanning is a very useful technique especially if you want to have a grasp or an overview of the content of the designated text that you have to read. Scanning is essential in knowing the entirety of a certain article and you do not really have to put focus on specific sections or details. Mainly, you just have to familiarize yourself with the overall "shape" of the reading material, the key topics or main issues, and other major characteristics of the text. Basically, when you are scanning a certain text, you are only tasked to look at the subtitles or subheadings included in the write-up. Usually, you have to point out key phrases and key words so as to give you a hint on what your text is focusing on. Usually, it helps if you will read the first few sentences of each paragraph. This way, you will have an idea on what the main points refer to as the discussion progresses.

To define, scanning is utilized to search for specific bits of information. Usually, a reader who scans uses his eyes to "hunt" for specific bits of knowledge and information that he needs. Scanning is usually done by office executives and their respective secretaries whenever they attend meetings, planning sessions, and draft schedules. Such details are useful in finding only the details that matter to them – nothing more and nothing less. In the process of scanning, if ever you find phrases or words that you are not familiar with, you do not have to worry.

Those who do scanning usually have a ready specific question in mind. Usually, scanning patterns are utilized. Some use the "winding S" or the "zigzag pattern" so that the eyes can move around quickly through the page. If what you are looking for is a proper name of a person, a place, or an event, then you might find the capital letters useful. If you are looking for specific dates or statistics, then you might want to look out for numbers or figures. In scanning, you only look for the information that you need.

Scanning – Some Practical Examples

(1) Looking for specific programs on the TV guide published on the newspaper

(2) Searching for the telephone number of your favorite restaurant in the directory

(3) Finding out what's in store for you today based on your Horoscope

Main Reading Technique #2: Focused Reading

There are two important skills that are employed as far as focused reading is concerned, namely: intensive and extensive reading. We will be discussing each in the next few paragraphs. Focused reading is all about establishing a specific area of focus or emphasis. In simpler terms, the purpose of reading is factored in and you have to fulfill that purpose. At this point, we will now differentiate Intensive reading from extensive reading.

(*) Intensive Reading: The technique of intensive reading can only be employed when dealing with short articles or write-ups. Here, you are guided with the goal or objective of extracting or coming up with very specific information. You have to employ your eyes in grasping specific details. In such cases, you have to gain a thorough understanding of all words that are used, numbers that cited, and facts that are included.

Intensive Reading – Some Practical Examples

(1) Reading a laboratory report in thermodynamics

(2) Understanding a newspaper article or an entry in an international journal

(3) Coming up with a response for a business letter

(*) Extensive Reading: In essence, extensive reading is mainly utilized to get a general kind of understanding of a certain topic or subject. Usually, long passages and articles that are read in the name of pleasure and recreation are included here. Experts say that books on business are also included here. Skills in extensive reading are generally used to enhance one's general familiarity on information about specific procedures. There is nothing to worry about if there are certain passages that are not familiar with you. You just have to skip that part and move on.

Extensive Reading – Some Practical Examples

(1) A book on accounting for non-accountants

(2) Your favorite epic novel that you read before you sleep

(3) A magazine article that caught your attention while drinking coffee

Main Reading Technique #3: Skimming

Finally, you also have to understand what skimming is. Strictly defined, "skimming" refers to the technique used in gathering only the "gist," summary, or the most essential information. One's eyes need to run through quickly in the text. Whenever you do skimming, you do not have to read each word, each phrase, or each sentence.

The general idea could be obtained through skimming. In a short period of time, you will be able to cover an entire chapter. Usually, whenever you wish to read a new book, you usually skim through chapters to decide if it is the next one that you will read. We all do skimming; we are just unaware that we are doing it. Note that details are not that important in this reading technique. If you are clueless about the procedures of skimming, here's a quick overview on how to do this:

First, you have to read the entire initial paragraph of the chapter you are interested to skim through to get the general orientation of the text. Then, you have to read all headings and subheadings or subtopics. Next, the first sentences of the paragraphs are read thoroughly. If there are any maps, charts, pictures, illustrations, or graphs, then you have to closely study them, too. Lastly, the final paragraph of the selection should be read completely. There are people who jot down notes or create an outline or article "skeleton" based on what they have skimmed.

Skimming – Some Practical Examples

(1) The entire newspaper (from cover to cover)

(2) The entire magazine

(3) Travel and business brochures

Chapter 2–Daily Routine Tips For Improving Reading Skills

Reading is a skill that you have to constantly hone, enhance, and improve. Improving one's skills in reading can be a bit challenging, but there are ways that can surely help you become better at it and steps that can help you catch up that reading habit.

Of course, it all begins with properly selecting great reading materials. As a beginner, you need to choose materials that are aligned with your interest. Additionally, a bad book will not help at all because it is like forcing yourself to eat something that you do not like. Hence, a good book will help you better appreciate the value of reading.

Here are some tips that can help you improve your skills in reading. Do these every single day and for sure, you will see improvement:

Routine Tip for Better Reading #1: Carry a book at all times

It does not matter where you go. By all means, carry a book with you. When you leave your house, put your favorite book in your bag. If you have a car, keep as many books as you can so that you can read anytime you want to.

Routine Tip for Better Reading #2: Create a reading wish list

There's actually a popular list – 100 books that you want to read before you die – you might want to check that out. Whenever there's a good book recommendation, take note of that. It is okay to create a long list of books. Someday, you will have enough time to read all the books that you want. This will motivate you to start reading and continue the drive to learn more.

Routine Tip for Better Reading #3: Set specific times within the day for reading

It does not matter if you will only devote ten to fifteen minutes or an hour or two before you sleep to reading. For as long as you will make it a regular habit, it is okay. Making sure that you are reading every single day will help keep your passion for reading burning.

Routine Tip for Better Reading #4: Cut down the time that you spend for television and the Internet

Instead of wasting your precious time on television shows or on Facebook or Twitter, why not spend it doing something more worthwhile? You will benefit more from reading, and there's no counterargument for that.

Routine Tip for Better Reading #5: Put it in your blog

One of the most popular ways of forming the reading habit is by putting up a blog. In ways more than one, reading is best complemented by writing. You do not have to spend a single penny blogging, so why not start right away? This will give you an additional push and motivation to read more.

Routine Tip for Better Reading #6: Prepare a quiet and comfortable space that is devoted for your reading

A quiet space offers you more reasons to spend time reading. This will help you proceed exploring your chosen reading material sans any form of interruptions. That space should have a comfortable chair and a table. If there is no such space at your home, you need to make one.

These are just some tips so that you will be encouraged to read more. Set high goals. Once you get the hang of it, you might not notice that you are already reading an average of fifty books per year. That's a pretty good number and that is not impossible to attain. Just be sure that you are enjoying what you are doing and that you are rushing your reading. Maintain the factor of pleasure and enjoyment by all means. Do it while you are eating your favorite food or drinking your favorite beverage. Do it while sitting on a comfy chair or while lying down on your bed. But most importantly, do it to increase your knowledge and to improve yourself.

Chapter 3–How To Determine What Is Important

A reader should have a keen eye to accurately identify the gist, the topic, and the main idea of a book's particular chapter, a journal entry's discussion of results, a single paragraph, a short news clip, or even a single sentence.

From there, you can easily draw important things like an evaluation, a conclusion, or a critical interpretation. This will gauge your overall understanding of the topic in particular and the entire article in general.

Before proceeding with the next part of the discussion, take note that the "topic" refers to a write-ups message, theme, or broad guide for writing the topic also stand for.

On the other hand, the main idea refers to the reading material's key concept.

Lastly, the details are the supporting ideas that can either be major or minorand are supplied in order to give necessary support to the chosen main idea. Such details are essential.

As a reader, you need to learn how to point out the topic, the main idea, and the details. These are the important elements of any reading material.

How can a reader determine the important points?

First, he needs to identify the key themes and ideas. Additionally, he needs to be able to distinguish between information and details that are important and unimportant. This can be done by relating the details or bits of information to the theme, main idea, or topic of the write-up. The level of importance of any information can also be determined by looking at how it is placed in the sentence or the paragraph or the text in general.

How can a reader determine whether a certain bit of information within the text is relevant or irrelevant?

First, readers need to remember that details vary in terms of importance. Therefore, they should be processed with varied levels of comprehension. A successful reader can readily discern which details are truly important and which ones are incidental.

Also, a reader always places the purpose of reading in the context. This definitely helps in assessing the importance of the details. Note that while the writer has an original intention when it comes to importance of details, there is a great possibility that the reader has his own interpretation of the text. Hence, the understanding of details can deviate from those that are aligned with the author's intent.

Chapter 4–How Speed Reading Is Related To Comprehension

Did you know that speed reading can only be successful if comprehension is attained? Speed reading is not only about the speed; it has something to do with understanding the material, too. Experts say that there is no such thing as a shortcut towards mastering speed reading. After all, it is not easy to master reading one thousand two hundred words within a span of sixty seconds.

On the average, a normal person can only read up to four hundred words within sixty seconds. If you are a speed reader, you usually fall within the following range: one thousand to one thousand seven hundred words per minute. In order to master speed reading without compromising comprehension, you might want to follow these important tips:

Speed Reading and Comprehension Tip #1: Classify reading materials according to importance and priority

Usually, there are three kinds of reading materials: very important, important, and the not-so important. Classify the reading materials that you have accordingly. After arranging, you can proceed with reading. This way, your level of comprehension will greatly improve because you get to encounter the most important materials first.

Speed Reading and Comprehension Tip #2: Do some skimming first

By skimming through the reading material first, you will be able to point out right away the main ideas and important points. Also, skimming can point out the orientation of your reading. Having an overview will help you become a more efficient reader.

Speed Reading and Comprehension Tip #3: Do your reading in an environment that is conducive for such activity

Aside from choosing a quiet corner, make sure that you are also maintaining the proper posture every time you read. Remember that ideally, you have to read using a bookstand. The angel of the reading material should be 45 degrees with respect to your eyes. This way, you can be sure that your speed of reading will be at the optimum, not to mention the fact that eyestrain is significantly reduced. Additionally, you have to assess if you are reading a certain type of material in the proper venue. For example, novels of recreation and leisure can be read in your bed, but it might not be a great idea to bring volumes of the encyclopedia in the same venue. Difficult readings should be done elsewhere (for example, in the library).

Speed Reading and Comprehension Tip #4: Jot down notes

The speed of reading can be greatly improved if you are capable of taking down notes properly. These notes can contain the important points or even questions. In time, you can choose to review the notes and address questions that you have written.

Speed Reading and Comprehension Tip #5: Read at a pace you are comfortable with

Usually, for different kinds of materials, there is a different kind of speed. For example, difficult readings might take more time to read, analyze, and process than light reading materials.

Chapter 5–Tips For Analyzing Paragraphs

Assignments and homework, especially of college students, often demand a great deal of analysis. Whenever you are asked to analyze, you are expected to make an inference or an interpretation. Therefore, if you want to analyze paragraphs, you have to understand that there is a need for critical thinking. Critical thinking is an essential skill that you can use in many aspects of your life. In this chapter, you will be given tips on how to analyze paragraphs.

Doing an Evaluation

When you are asked to do an evaluation, you have to make a decision on whether something is good or bad, worthy or unworthy, accurate or inaccurate, correct or incorrect, among others. For example, if you watched a movie and you are asked to do an evaluation, then you have to evaluate whether that movie is worth watching or otherwise. When asked to evaluate a reading material, you have to judge its elements. Was it well-written in terms of grammar and mechanics? What is your opinion about its overall value as a written piece? These are some of the questions that you might want to answer when making an evaluation.

Creating an Inference

When asked to make an inference, it means that you have to analyze the situation and give the meaning of something that has not been stated in an explicit manner in the text. This is another mode of analysis because one has to do a great deal of thought to successfully perform this. Usually, "making an inference" is synonymous to "reading between and beyond the lines."

Interpreting what you have read

Usually, if you are asked to interpret anything that you have read, you have to state the meaning of the reading material assigned to you with the use of your own words. Usually, an interpretation of a lengthy reading material consists of only a few sentences. You simply have to express the message of the material assigned to you. Usually, interpretations are very personal so it is quite easy to justify such interpretations.

Chapter 6–The Importance Of Increasing Your Vocabulary

One reads in order to improve his vocabulary. But did you know that there are people who are making conscious efforts to improve their vocabulary so that they can be better readers?

If you will ask ten of your friends this question, perhaps only a few will answer with a smile: "Are you truly satisfied and comfortable with your vocabulary?" Try asking yourself the same question. Now, do you feel bad about your answer?

Having a broad vocabulary has many advantages. At this point, let us point out the different benefits of a good vocabulary. First, it enables you to communicate well and to be an effective conveyor of information. Additionally, a good vocabulary can help improve you level of confidence, self-worth, and self-esteem. Other people try to study more words so that they will sound more sophisticated and knowledgeable. Also, people who have better vocabulary are statistically favored to have better kinds of job offers. Finally, an improved vocabulary can lead to improved perception of other people.

A limited vocabulary may lead other people to believe that you are uneducated. Of course, such a perception has its disadvantages, and that is what we are trying to avoid. Aside from that, in the context of reading, you will find it easier to understand any discussion – regardless of the nature of the reading material. With a wide vocabulary, you will feel smarter and you will feel truly confident. Your command of the knowledge truly has an effect on how good a reader you are.

Please remember that when you are reading a book or any material for that matter, you will not always have an access to a dictionary. To avoid the constant need for a dictionary or an interpreter, try to enrich your vocabulary.

Chapter 7 –Proper Vision Techniques And Eye Movement

Proper techniques in terms of vision and mastering the proper movement of the eyes in reading are also components of an essential step in getting that reading habit. The movement of the eyes has a great influence in the brain's visual processing of the text being read. According to researchers, the eyes, during the process of reading, do not make continuous movements through the lines. Instead, they perform a lot of saccades or rapid and short lateral movements which are cut short by fixations or short stops in between.

You might be thinking that it is not important to know much about this because it is a natural thing, but on the contrary, proper knowledge about eye movements will help you further enhance your reading speed, which in turn will optimize your level of comprehension. Additionally, if ever you are having difficulty with reading, this aspect might be explored to find out if there are any abnormalities or irregularities when it comes to how your eyes are moving while you are reading.

Nowadays, it is quite easy to track the motion of the eyes while reading. With the use of technology which is further aided by machines and computers, the movements of a person's eyes can be easily tracked. Computers can now efficiently record *anything* and that includes eye movements. From the findings, one's eye movements can be traced and better understood.

What exactly are saccades? Strictly speaking, saccades can be defined as the movement of the eyes in the horizontal fashion. Usually, the direction taken by saccades is from left to right. Readers who are of superior skill can move their eyes at a very fast rate. The eyes usually stop to process acquired information. Usually, the fixation period lasts only for a very small fraction of a second, after which, the reader performs another saccade. A saccade usually covers a short and swift movement within a span of an average of seven to nine characters.

The rate of reading usually varies due to the difference in the length of time devoted by a reader to his saccades and fixations. Usually, slow readers find it difficult to make a transition from a fixation to a new saccade. For other slow readers, the problem lies with the regression.

In the end, any reader must understand that the movement of the eyes and the rate by which a reader is able to do that has a great influence in the intellectual and cognitive processing of the information acquired.

Chapter 8–Strategies For Improving Your Reading Comprehension

Improving comprehension level can be done. It is possible if you know the strategies and if you will apply them whenever you are in a reading situation. Here are some techniques that were tried and tested by experts:

(*) *Try to read the most important stuff right after you wake up.* Studies show that the brain is well-rested when you wake up in the morning and it can take in any information that is presented to it. Therefore, this is the best time to read.

(*) *Do reading in short, solid, and uninterrupted intervals.* For example, try reading between half to quarter of an hour without any breaks. After that, rest for a minute or two and then resume reading again. That way, you can assure that you have the focus and at the same time, you can be sure with the quality of your reading.

(*) *As previously pointed out, location matters.* As much as possible, avoid halls that are frequented by many people. Try to find a corner wherein you won't be disturbed by anyone. The bottom line is that you need to find a spot that is conducive for reading.

(*) *From time to time, ask yourself self-check questions to monitor your level of comprehension.* Ask yourself: "What information and knowledge have I acquired so far?"

(*) *Annotate the reading material.* By putting highlights on important phrases, by encircling significant points, or underlining names of people, and by writing notes on the margin, you can be sure that you are improving your level of understanding of what you are reading.

(*) *Begin by skimming before doing your focused reading.* This will help you become better oriented of the topic.

There are two methods that are recommended by developmental reading experts so that you can become a full-fledged active reader:

Active Reading Method #1: The Cornell Method

The Cornell Method, more popularly known as the SQ3R method, stands for Survey, Question, Read, Review, and Recite. Each of these words is quite self-explanatory. By following these steps, you will become a better reader who is known for gaining thorough understanding of the materials that he is reading.

Active Reading Method #2: Compose your questions

On a piece of paper, create two columns. The first column will be devoted to questions that you formulate. The second column will be for the answers. Creating questions will give you an additional push to explore and understand the reading material assigned to you.

Actually, there are many other methods, but these are two of the most practical and the most effective methods that have been proven to help in improving comprehension levels.

Chapter 9–Speed Reading Tricks And Tips

This final chapter is devoted to tips and tricks on how to improve your speed reading skills. It all begins with practice, but there are sever areas that you have to focus on and those areas will be discussed in this chapter.

Speed Reading Tip #1: Never repeat

Move on and move forward by all means. Repeating does nothing but slow you down. If you wish to read fast, only read it once and never try to read it again in your head because it will significantly slow you down. Also, try to read using your eyes and not with your mouth. Such redundancy will make your speed and efficiency suffer.

Speed Reading Tip #2: Use your finger as your eyes' guide for reading

The rationale here is that your finger can help guide your eyes run through a pre-determined path. The finger can set the pace and it can help you have a better understanding of what you are currently reading

Speed Reading Tip #3: Concentrate and never lose your focus

The point of this tip is quite simple, but it is worth including in the list. Speed reading will definitely be a chore if you don't concentrate. You will repeatedly find yourself in the middle of confusion if you constantly lose your focus.

Speed Reading Tip #4: Follow the "Third Word Rule" at all times

The rule is simple: start reading on the third word of the line and end reading on the third to the last word of the line. Once you religiously follow this, you will find out that you still get to understand what you are reading even if you are not reading each line completely. How is this possible? Simple – you are maximizing your peripherals.

Speed Reading Tip #5: Read phrases and lines, not individual words

Therefore, it is pointless to hold the book to close to your face. The minimum distance should be at least two feet away from your face. By doing this, you will be able to read at least three words at a time.

Speed Reading Tip #6: Never go back

Trust yourself that you have gathered enough information. Never attempt to go back and repeat what you have already read. The brain has its ways to fill the in-betweens in case you think that you missed something.

Speed Reading Tip #7: Gain momentum by beginning at maximum speed

If you are beginning your reading with a very fast pace, comprehension will be easier, studies show. You will begin to be comfortable with the speed and with time, it will still improve.

Please note that speed reading cannot be mastered overnight. You have to spend time practicing and honing your interest in reading. Constant practice and application is the key, so do not even dare try to spend days without reading. With constant practice and exposure, you will get the hang of it.

Conclusion

Thank you again for purchasing this book on reading comprehension and speed reading techniques!

I am extremely excited to pass this information along to you, and I am so happy that you now have read and can hopefully implement these strategies going forward.

I hope this book was able to help you understand the concept behind reading comprehension success and how to further improve your speed reading skills.

The next step is to get started using this information and to hopefully live a productive and enjoyable kind of life that is ready to take on the challenge of expanding your knowledge base through reading!

Please don't be someone who just reads this information and doesn't apply it, the strategies in this book will only benefit you if you use them!

If you know of anyone else that could benefit from the information presented here please inform them of this book.

Finally, if you enjoyed this book and feel it has added value to your life in any way, please take the time to share your thoughts and post a review on Amazon. It'd be greatly appreciated!

Thank you and good luck!

Preview Of:

<u>Success Secrets</u>

Powerful Success Secrets Of NLP, Meditation, And Self Hypnosis To Improve Relationships, Succeed In Business, Increase Emotional Intelligence And Health!

Introduction

I want to thank you and congratulate you for purchasing the book, *"Success Secrets: Powerful Success Secrets Of NLP, Meditation, And Self Hypnosis To Improve Relationships, Succeed In Business, Increase Emotional Intelligence And Health!"*.

Success Secrets To Succeed In Life!

"Success Secrets" contains success secrets on how to incorporate NLP, Meditation, and Self Hypnosis into your life to create better relationships, succeed in business and building wealth, increase your emotional intelligence and control over your feelings, and attract better health!

The mind is an unbelievably powerful tool that we have at our disposal, we can attract good into our lives just as easy as we can attract bad! When you think about this it sounds a little scary. The mere thought that you could be manifesting negativity, scarcity, ill health, and other bad things really can freak you out! But stop! That is not the point; in fact, this is why we need to learn these techniques in the first place! So we stop thinking and bringing things we don't want, and start encouraging things we do!

There are so many things that your mind can do to bring success to your life. All you need to do is to find out what these things are. Successful people must be doing something different in their life that contributes to their success. If you want to be successful, you should find out what these success secrets are and use them to your advantage.

You can learn about the secrets to success using your mind power by reading this book. It focuses on different aspects of your life such as your relationships, career or business, health, and emotional intelligence.

Thanks again for purchasing this book, I hope you enjoy it!

Chapter 1: Successful People Have Success Secrets

Before you learn about the different success secrets involving the use of NLP, meditation, and self hypnosis, you first need to recognize that successful people have success secrets. These secrets to success set them apart from the rest – from those who are still trying to achieve their dreams and goals in life.

There are a lot of famous successful people that you hear and read about in the news on TV or the internet or in published books and magazines. Forbes, for example, makes a list of the most successful or powerful people in terms of their gross income and their influence and legacy. There are successful people in their chosen fields like sports, business, entertainment, among others. You know about Bill Gates, George Soros, and Warren Buffet. You know so many other people who are considered successful in their life. So what makes these people successful? What can you learn from them that you can use to reach your own dreams and aspirations in life?

One thing that these highly successful people have in common is their superior brain power. It does not necessarily mean that they performed extremely well in academics, although that can be an advantage. It means that they know how to use the power of their mind to achieve what they want to achieve in life. Some of these successful people did not have lots of money to start their business with. They just had the right idea, vision, and the right frame of mind and also the right mind power formula that brought them to where they are right now. You need to understand that having the right idea or knowledge is not enough. You also need to know how to utilize your mind power to help you turn this idea into reality.

These successful people were in difficult situations before they became successful on their own merits. Some already had the money, education, and connection that they needed while others were not fortunate enough. Either way, these people use mind techniques that help them reach their destination in life. They apply superior mind formulas that worked well with their ideas and plans. The good thing about this is that these mind formulas can be learned. It is not something that your parents can pass on to you or something that you learn from the traditional school. Bill Gates, Warren Buffet, and George Soros learned how to use their mind skills that made them successful in their chosen industries.

Everything that you do, feel, and think is connected to your mind. Your mind plays an important role in your perspectives and experiences in life. You need to acquire how these successful people view the world or how they act when faced with challenges that can help you become like them. The mind is powerful, everyone knows that. But only a few knows how to utilize this power to improve their lives. This is the secret to success, learning how to use the power of the mind to achieve your goals and ambitions in life.

Thanks for Previewing My Exciting Book Entitled:

"Success Secrets: Powerful Success Secrets Of NLP, Meditation, And Self Hypnosis To Improve Relationships, Succeed In Business, Increase Emotional Intelligence And Health!"

To purchase this book, simply go to the Amazon Kindle store and simply search:

"SUCCESS SECRETS"

Then just scroll down until you see my book. You will know it is mine because you will see my name "Ryan Cooper" underneath the title.

Alternatively, you can visit my author page on Amazon to see this book and other work I have done. Thanks so much, and please don't forget your free bonuses

DON'T LEAVE YET! - CHECK OUT YOUR FREE BONUSES BELOW!

Free Bonus Offer 1: Get Free Access To The OperationAwesomeLife.com VIP Newsletter!

Free Bonus Offer 2: Get A Free Download Of My Friends Amazing Book "Passive Income" First Chapter!

Free Bonus Offer 3: Get A Free Email Series On Making Money Online When You Join Newsletter!

GET ALL 3 FREE

Once you enter your email address you will immediately get free access to this awesome **VIP NEWSLETTER**!

For a limited time, if you join for free right now, you will also get free access to the first chapter of the awesome book "**PASSIVE INCOME**"!

And, last but definitely not least, if you join the newsletter right now, you also will get a free 10 part email series on **10 SUCCESS SECRETS OF MAKING MONEY ONLINE!**

To claim all 3 of your FREE BONUSES just click below!

Just Go Here for all 3 VIP bonuses!

OperationAwesomeLife.com

Made in the USA
Middletown, DE
23 November 2019